Baby Animals in the Wild!

Rabbit Kits in the Wild

by Katie Chanez

Bullfrog Books

Ideas for Parents and Teachers

Bullfrog Books let children practice reading informational text at the earliest reading levels. Repetition, familiar words, and photo labels support early readers.

Before Reading
- Discuss the cover photo. What does it tell them?
- Look at the picture glossary together. Read and discuss the words.

Read the Book
- "Walk" through the book and look at the photos. Let the child ask questions. Point out the photo labels.
- Read the book to the child, or have him or her read independently.

After Reading
- Prompt the child to think more. Ask: Rabbit kits are born in a nest. Can you name any other baby animals that are born in nests?

Bullfrog Books are published by Jump!
5357 Penn Avenue South
Minneapolis, MN 55419
www.jumplibrary.com

Copyright © 2024 Jump! International copyright reserved in all countries. No part of this book may be reproduced in any form without written permission from the publisher.

Library of Congress Cataloging-in-Publication Data

Names: Chanez, Katie, author.
Title: Rabbit kits in the wild / by Katie Chanez.
Description: Minneapolis, MN: Jump!, Inc., [2024]
Series: Baby animals in the wild! | Includes index.
Audience: Ages 5–8
Identifiers: LCCN 2022043064 (print)
LCCN 2022043065 (ebook)
ISBN 9798885244091 (hardcover)
ISBN 9798885244107 (paperback)
ISBN 9798885244114 (ebook)
Subjects: LCSH: Rabbits—Infancy—Juvenile literature.
Classification: LCC QL737.L32 C43 2024 (print)
LCC QL737.L32 (ebook)
DDC 599.3213/92—dc23/eng/20221223
LC record available at https://lccn.loc.gov/2022043064
LC ebook record available at https://lccn.loc.gov/2022043065

Editor: Eliza Leahy
Designer: Molly Ballanger

Photo Credits: Elena Elisseeva/Shutterstock, cover, 22 (kit), 24; Brad Sauter/Dreamstime, 1; CLS Digital Arts/Shutterstock, 3 (rabbit); Alexander Sviridov/Shutterstock, 3 (kit); JustStockPhotos/Alamy, 4; Christopher R Mazza/iStock, 5, 23bl; Wayne Wolfersberger/Shutterstock, 6; Scott Camazine/Alamy, 6–7, 23br; bradwieland iStock, 8; tracielouise/iStock, 9, 12–13, 14, 22 (tail), 23tl, 23tr; imageBROKER/Alamy, 10–11; Eric Isselee/Shutterstock, 15; Kirk Hewlett/Alamy, 16–17; Orchidpoet/iStock, 18–19; Susan Hodgson/Shutterstock, 20–21.

Printed in the United States of America at Corporate Graphics in North Mankato, Minnesota.

Table of Contents

Hop and Run	4
Parts of a Rabbit Kit	22
Picture Glossary	23
Index	24
To Learn More	24

Hop and Run

What is in this nest?

nest

kit

They are baby rabbits!
We call them kits.
Their eyes are closed.

Mom made the nest with grass and fur.

It is in the ground.

The kits stay warm in it.

Mom

The kits drink Mom's milk.
They grow fast.
Their eyes open.

They come out of the nest.
Their fur is fluffy.

fur

They hop.

They play.

They chase each other!

ear

One kit stops.
It hears something.

Look out!

It is a red fox.

The kit runs fast!

It hides under a bush.
It is safe.

The kit grows up.
It lives on its own.
Bye, rabbit!

Parts of a Rabbit Kit

What are the parts of a rabbit kit? Take a look!

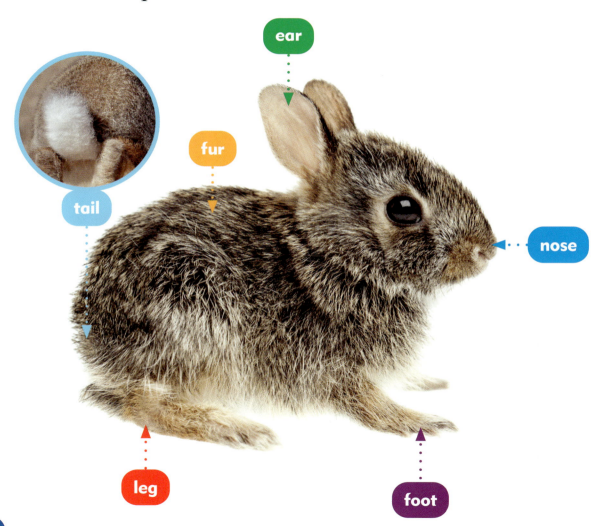

Picture Glossary

chase
To run after someone or something.

fluffy
Covered with soft, fine hair or fur.

kits
Baby rabbits.

nest
A place built by an animal to live in and care for its young.

Index

eyes 5, 8
fur 6, 9
grass 6
grow 8, 21
hears 14
hides 18

hop 11
milk 8
nest 4, 6, 9
play 12
red fox 15
runs 17

To Learn More

Finding more information is as easy as 1, 2, 3.

❶ Go to www.factsurfer.com

❷ Enter "rabbitkits" into the search box.

❸ Choose your book to see a list of websites.